First published in 2005

Copyright © text John Long, 2005
Copyright © illustrations Brian Choo, 2005
Copyright © maps Sergei Pisarevsky, 2005
For a complete list of images and acknowledgements,
please see page 47

Allen & Unwin
83 Alexander St
Crows Nest NSW 2065
Australia
Phone: (61 2) 8425 0100
Fax: (61 2) 9906 2218
Email: info@allenandunwin.com
Web: www.allenandunwin.com
Distributed in the UK, Eire and Europe
by Frances Lincoln Ltd, London NW5 2RZ

National Library of Australia
Cataloguing-in-Publication entry:

Long, John A., 1957- .
The big picture book.

For children.
Includes index.
ISBN 1 74114 328 4.

1. Evolution (biology) - Juvenile literature. 2. Life -
Origin - Juvenile literature. 3. Natural history -
Juvenile literature. I. Choo, Brian. II. Pisarevsky,
Sergei. III. Title.

576.8

Cover and text design by Patricia Howes

10 9 8 7 6 5 4 3 2 1

Teachers' notes available from www.allenandunwin.com

THE BIG PICTURE BOOK

See life on Earth unfolding through time

JOHN LONG

Illustrations by **Brian Choo**

and maps by Sergei Pisarevsky

ALLEN&UNWIN

In each of us, both you and me,
there is a little piece of a star.
For we are made of atoms formed
at the beginning of time,
at the very birth of the Universe ...

1 000 000 000
years ago

2 000 000 000
years ago

3 000 000 000
years ago

4 000 000 000
years ago

5 000 000 000
years ago

6 000 000 000
years ago

7 000 000 000
years ago

8 000 000 000
years ago

9 000 000 000
years ago

10 000 000 000
years ago

11 000 000 000
years ago

12 000 000 000
years ago

12,000,000,000 years ago

12 billion years ago ...

The Universe formed out of clouds of gases
(or was it always there —
everywhere atoms buzzing with energy?).
Did it explode into existence, in an instant Big Bang,
infinitely hot, bigger than imagining?
Or was there no beginning,
just an 'always is'?
Scientists wonder and argue.

The Universe is a mystery.
The beginning of all things is a mystery.

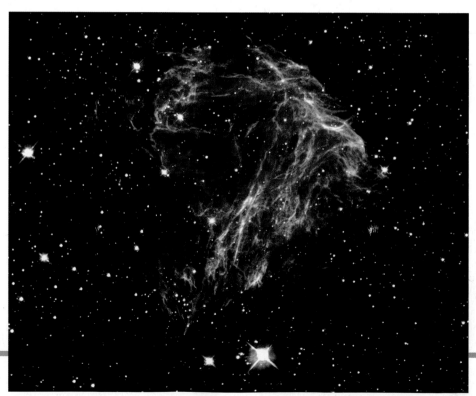

▲ An exploded star, a nebula, is a way for us to look back in time and to see how the universe once formed.

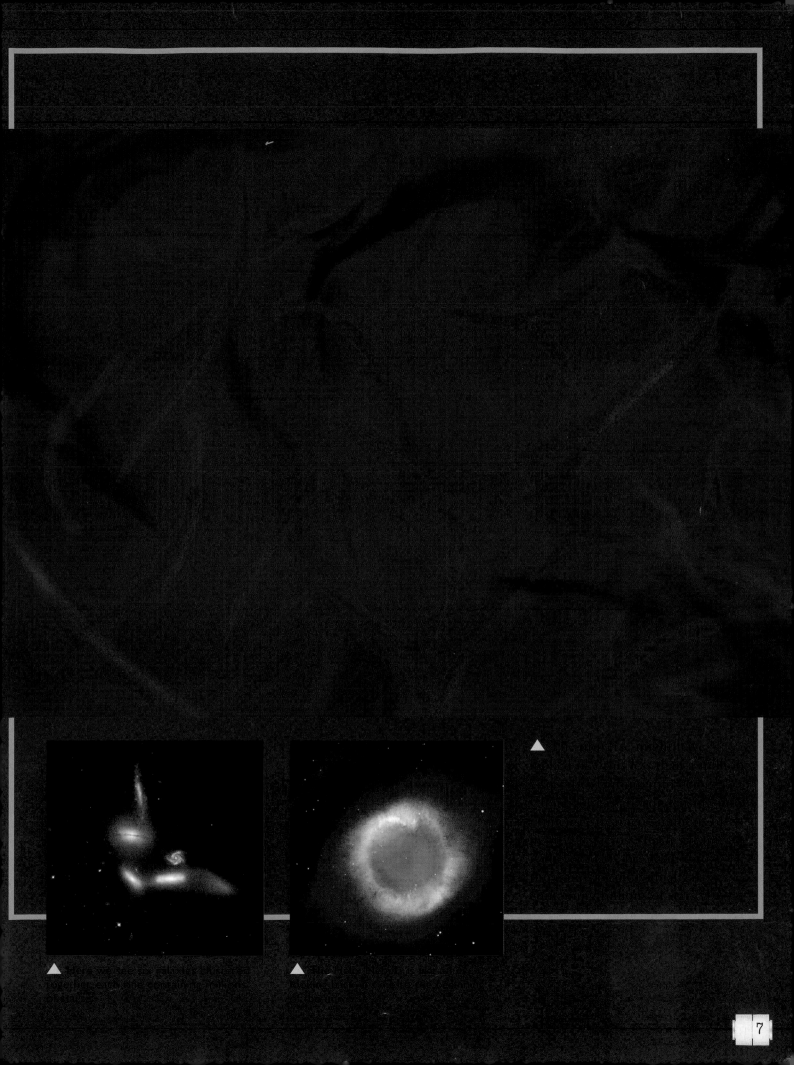

▲ Here we see 20 galaxies clustered
together, each one containing millions...

▲ This is a planetary nebula called the
Helix...

TODAY

1 000 000 000
years ago

2 000 000 000
years ago

3 000 000 000
years ago

4 000 000 000
years ago

5 000 000 000
years ago

6 000 000 000
years ago

7 000 000 000
years ago

8 000 000 000
years ago

9 000 000 000
years ago

10 000 000 000
years ago

11 000 000 000
years ago

12 000 000 000
years ago

4,500,000,000 years ago

Four and half billion years ago ...

Earth was born.
A massive rotating cloud of hot gases
(the debris of exploded stars)
cooled, slowly, slowly, over billions of years
to form the sun and planets.
Still Earth's surface was fiery, hotter than we can think.
It was made of lava and poisonous gas;
there was nowhere cool enough for solid rock to exist.

Earth was born, and yet life was not.

◀ An asteroid, like a planet, is composed of stone and metals.

▶ A meteorite is composed mostly of iron and nickel, the metals that also make up the core of planets like Earth.

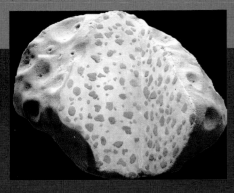

▲ The young Earth is a world of molten rock being continually bombarded by meteors. The temperature of the planet is just beginning to drop to a point where a solid crust forms, but it will be hundreds of millions of years before it is cool enough for there to be any water.

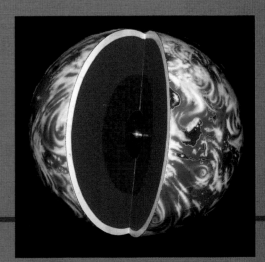

▲ The sun, photographed with a filter around its edges, shows the huge extent of the solar flares that reach far out into space. The sun is one of billions of stars in the Universe.

▲ A cross-section of our planet Earth. We live on the crust, the thin outer shell.

TODAY

1 000 000 000
years ago

2 000 000 000
years ago

3 000 000 000
years ago

4 000 000 000
years ago

5 000 000 000
years ago

6 000 000 000
years ago

7 000 000 000
years ago

8 000 000 000
years ago

9 000 000 000
years ago

10 000 000 000
years ago

11 000 000 000
years ago

12 000 000 000
years ago

3,500,000,000 years ago

Three and a half billion years ago ...

First life appeared.
The Earth was cool enough for oceans to form.
Groups of atoms called molecules could reproduce,
and make copies of themselves.
So life appeared in the seas.
These single-celled bacteria caught floating sand grains
and the grains built up over millennia into mounds,
now hardened into rock.
We call these mounds stromatolites.
They still live today in some quiet coves.

So life came to Earth in a small way, quietly.

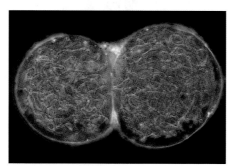

▲ Cells of cyanobacteria, like these, are
amongst the most primitive of all life.

▶ These brilliantly coloured layers of
3.5-billion-year-old sediment from
Western Australia were made by single-
celled cyanobacteria binding grains of
sand together to form stromatolites.

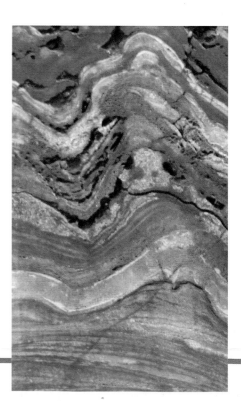

▲ Fields of stromatolites lie exposed at low tide in a shallow bay. Each dome is a colony built up by the actions of countless individual cyanobacteria. Over 3 billion years later, these structures will be preserved in the remote Pilbara region of Western Australia.

▲ A colony of living stromatolites at Lake Clifton, Western Australia. Today stromatolites live in both marine and freshwater habitats.

TODAY

1 000 000 000
years ago

2 000 000 000
years ago

3 000 000 000
years ago

4 000 000 000
years ago

5 000 000 000
years ago

6 000 000 000
years ago

7 000 000 000
years ago

8 000 000 000
years ago

9 000 000 000
years ago

10 000 000 000
years ago

11 000 000 000
years ago

12 000 000 000
years ago

2,100,000,000 years ago

Just over two billion years ago ...

Life took on new forms.
The first single-celled life with a nucleus appeared,
and multiplied.
One grew and grew, in a spiral,
a seaweed spiral we now call *Grypania*.
Over time, life changed shape.

It was a great step in Earth's history
when cells began to multiply and change.

A colourful section of rock called a banded iron formation. These rocks developed in Western Australia over 2 billion years ago, at a time when the seas were rich in iron and the atmosphere was abundant in oxygen. The seas 'rusted' and iron-rich sediments dropped to the sea floor. Today they are a source of iron ore.

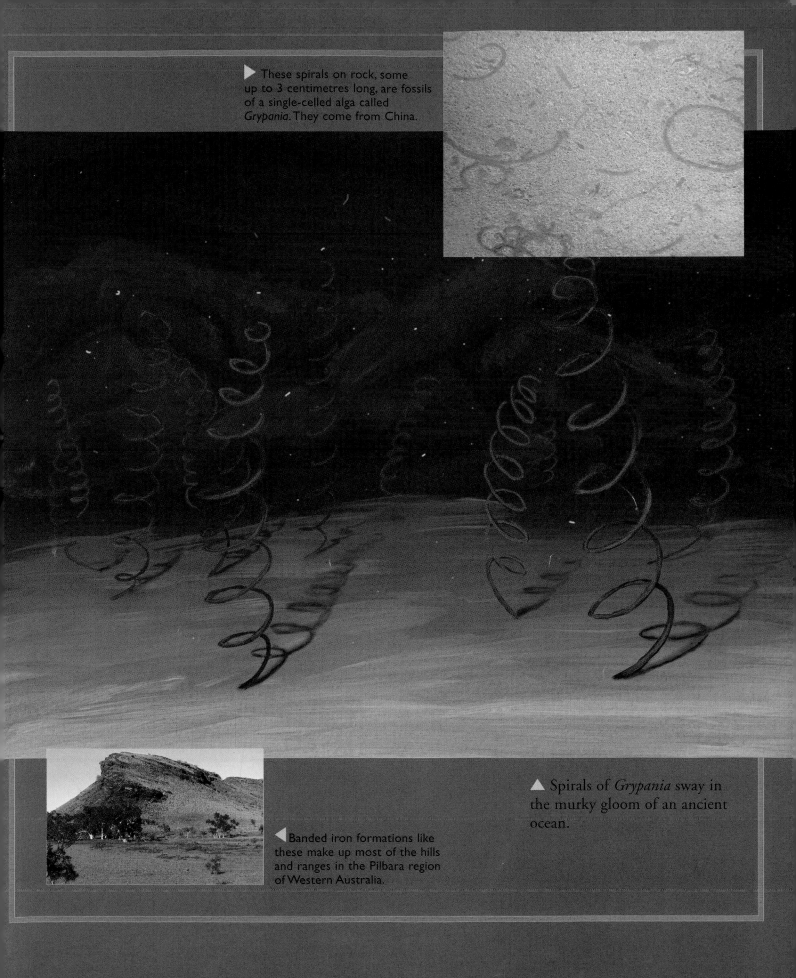

These spirals on rock, some up to 3 centimetres long, are fossils of a single-celled alga called *Grypania*. They come from China.

Banded iron formations like these make up most of the hills and ranges in the Pilbara region of Western Australia.

Spirals of *Grypania* sway in the murky gloom of an ancient ocean.

1 000 000 000
years ago

2 000 000 000
years ago

3 000 000 000
years ago

4 000 000 000
years ago

5 000 000 000
years ago

6 000 000 000
years ago

7 000 000 000
years ago

8 000 000 000
years ago

9 000 000 000
years ago

10 000 000 000
years ago

11 000 000 000
years ago

12 000 000 000
years ago

1,000,000,000 years ago

One billion years ago ...

Earth's landmass was in one piece,
a supercontinent we've named Rodinia.
Rodinia's surface was rock, sand and gas.
Life was only in the seas.
Organisms made up of many cells appeared
and grew larger than ever before.
Seaweeds like strands of beads
washed up on ancient seashores.

It was a great step in Earth's history
when many cells lived as one.

Seaweeds are kinds of algae which take in nutrients from the sea and energy from sunlight.

An eerie seashore scene, 1 billion years ago, when the land was utterly barren and lifeless. But in the sea and along the shore you would find strands of seaweed and the dome-like mounds of stromatolites.

These fossilised impressions show where balls of algae once rested on an ancient sandy shoreline. They were found near Newman, in Western Australia, and are just over 1 billion years old.

A strand of seaweed showing its branching structure with leaf-like bulbs at one end.

How the world looked about a billion years ago. The ancient supercontinent is called Rodinia.

1 000 000 000
years ago

2 000 000 000
years ago

3 000 000 000
years ago

4 000 000 000
years ago

5 000 000 000
years ago

6 000 000 000
years ago

7 000 000 000
years ago

8 000 000 000
years ago

9 000 000 000
years ago

10 000 000 000
years ago

11 000 000 000
years ago

12 000 000 000
years ago

560,000,000 years ago

Five hundred and sixty million years ago ...

The first animals had appeared.
Many wonderful creatures lived in the seas:
big jellyfish, sea pens and flat, round worms;
the first animal with a hard shell;
and others stranger then strange,
unlike anything we know.

It was a great step in Earth's history
when animals of different shapes and sizes
lived together!

A living jellyfish. These beautiful animals are metazoans (made up of many cells).

This fossil jellyfish, 20 centimetres wide, was preserved as an impression when sands covered it on an ancient shore. It was found in Ediacara, South Australia.

In a shallow sea off South Australia 560 million years ago, giant flatworms called *Dickinsonia* crawl on the sandy bottom while an enigmatic creature called *Tribrachidium* (far left) sits alone. The red leaves of *Charniodiscus* wave in the currents as they sift particles of food from the water.

This is an impression of a small *Dickinsonia*, a flatworm from Ediacara, South Australia. The biggest creatures of this age, some flatworms are as much as 1 metre long.

Continental landmasses as Rodinia was splitting up.

1 000 000 000
years ago

2 000 000 000
years ago

3 000 000 000
years ago

4 000 000 000
years ago

5 000 000 000
years ago

6 000 000 000
years ago

7 000 000 000
years ago

8 000 000 000
years ago

9 000 000 000
years ago

10 000 000 000
years ago

11 000 000 000
years ago

12 000 000 000
years ago

530,000,000 years ago

Five hundred and thirty million years ago ...

A smaller supercontinent called Gondwana
broke away from Rodinia.
New life forms sprang up everywhere.
Many animals grew hard shells.
Trilobites scurried over the world's first reefs,
corals and sponges lived next to snails and clams.
Savage hunters swam in the shadows,
chasing the first animals with bones, the fish.

This was a great step in Earth's history
when the first fish, our distant ancestors, arrived.

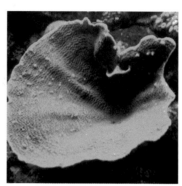

▲ A coral, one of the many
groups of animals that first
appeared at this time.

▲ A colourful sea anemone, one of the many
diverse life forms we find in the sea today.
They belong to the coelenterates, a group that
includes all jellyfish and corals.

◀ A fossilised trilobite from Morocco. Some
trilobites of this age reached 50 centimetres
in length.

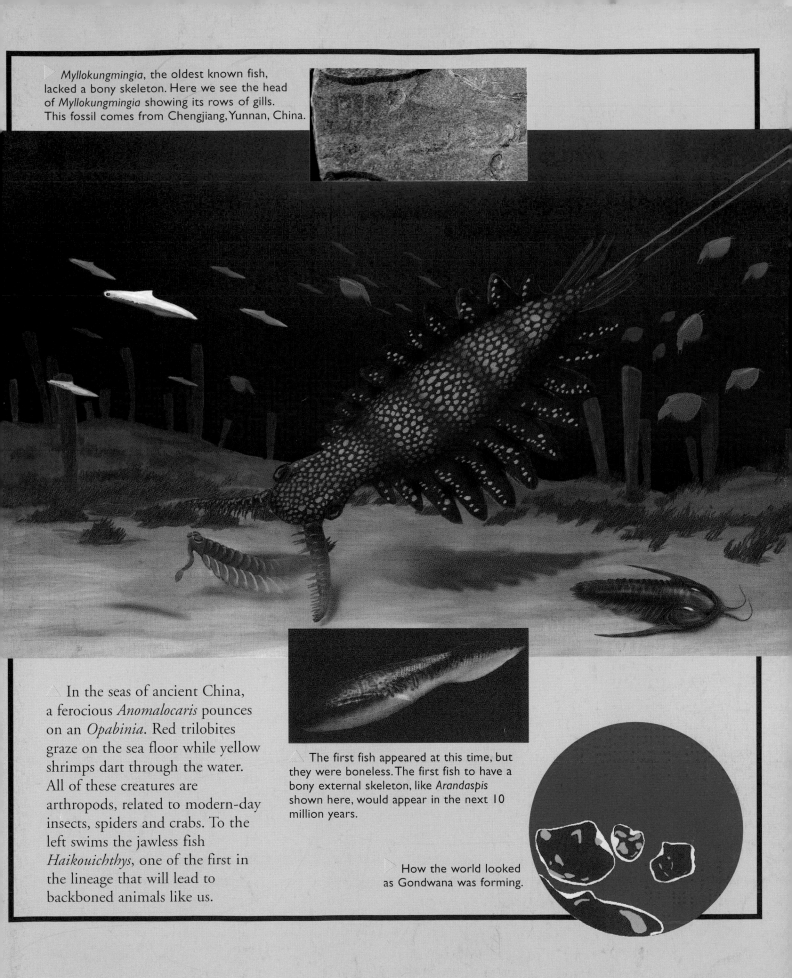

▷ *Myllokungmingia*, the oldest known fish, lacked a bony skeleton. Here we see the head of *Myllokungmingia* showing its rows of gills. This fossil comes from Chengjiang, Yunnan, China.

△ In the seas of ancient China, a ferocious *Anomalocaris* pounces on an *Opabinia*. Red trilobites graze on the sea floor while yellow shrimps dart through the water. All of these creatures are arthropods, related to modern-day insects, spiders and crabs. To the left swims the jawless fish *Haikouichthys*, one of the first in the lineage that will lead to backboned animals like us.

△ The first fish appeared at this time, but they were boneless. The first fish to have a bony external skeleton, like *Arandaspis* shown here, would appear in the next 10 million years.

▷ How the world looked as Gondwana was forming.

1 000 000 000
years ago

2 000 000 000
years ago

3 000 000 000
years ago

4 000 000 000
years ago

5 000 000 000
years ago

6 000 000 000
years ago

7 000 000 000
years ago

8 000 000 000
years ago

9 000 000 000
years ago

10 000 000 000
years ago

11 000 000 000
years ago

12 000 000 000
years ago

440,000,000 years ago

Four hundred and forty million years ago ...

There was life on land!
Tiny mites and spider-like creatures left the sea
and explored the barren land.
Simple plants without leaves
soon appeared on shore as well.
Giant sea scorpions ventured out of rivers
to walk upon sandy shores,
leaving huge trackways that would one day
be preserved as fossils in rock.

It was a great step in Earth's history
when living things first invaded the land.

A fossil of a sea scorpion or eurypterid from New York State, North America. These animals lived in the sea but occasionally made short walks onto land and left their trackways as fossil footprints in sandstone. This fossil is around 430 million years old.

On a Western Australian riverbank, 440 million years ago, a pair of fearsome eurypterids are too busy sparring with one another to notice the little *Kalbarria* scuttling towards the water. The trackways made by these arthropods are some of the earliest evidence for life on land.

This fossil is an impression of a creature having eleven pairs of legs, called a euthycarcinoid. The fossil, approximately 420 million years old, comes from Kalbarri in Western Australia.

At this time the supercontinent Gondwana centred on the South Pole, with most other large landmasses also in the southern hemisphere.

A living wolf spider. Close relatives of spiders called trigonotarbids were amongst the first creatures to inhabit the land.

1 000 000 000
years ago

2 000 000 000
years ago

3 000 000 000
years ago

4 000 000 000
years ago

5 000 000 000
years ago

6 000 000 000
years ago

7 000 000 000
years ago

8 000 000 000
years ago

9 000 000 000
years ago

10 000 000 000
years ago

11 000 000 000
years ago

12 000 000 000
years ago

400,000,000 years ago

Four hundred million years ago ...

Fish of many different shapes and sizes
swam in all the seas, rivers and lakes.
Strange jawless fish sifted mud,
looking for food on the sea bed.
Sharks with teeth and jaws chased smaller fish.
Giant placoderm fish ruled the seas and rivers.
Some fish had strong skeletons
with powerful fins to help them turn sharply.
Others had sharp spines to ward off enemies.

This was the next big step in Earth's history,
when fish first developed jaws with teeth.

This fossil is *Cheiracanthus*, an acanthodian fish from Scotland that lived about 385 million years ago. Many kinds of early fish had sharp spines as protection against predators.

The bony skull of an armoured placoderm fish from Wyoming, North America

A dagger-toothed fish, *Onychodus*, which lived around 380 million years ago, highlights the dramatic appearance of jaws and teeth. This was another important step in evolution, enabling early fish to catch and eat their prey effectively.

Weird fish swim in Chinese seas of 400 million years ago. In the foreground a spike-toothed *Psarolepis* harasses a school of jawless *Polybranchiaspis*. Two armoured placoderms called *Phymolepis* swim in the middle distance, while the giant *Youngolepis* and two tiny acanthodians cruise in the background.

A tiger shark. Sharks are primitive fish that lack bone, having instead a rubbery cartilage skeleton. Sharks are amongst the oldest known jawed fish.

Four hundred million years ago, there were two giant southern supercontinents, Gondwana and Euramerica.

This fossil fish, *Glyptolepis*, from Scotland, is a good example of a great step forward in evolution, the development of a strong internal skeleton.

1 000 000 000
years ago

2 000 000 000
years ago

3 000 000 000
years ago

4 000 000 000
years ago

5 000 000 000
years ago

6 000 000 000
years ago

7 000 000 000
years ago

8 000 000 000
years ago

9 000 000 000
years ago

10 000 000 000
years ago

11 000 000 000
years ago

12 000 000 000
years ago

370,000,000 years ago

Three hundred and seventy million years ago ...

Large trees grew skywards, and forests spread.
Huge dragonflies flew in misty skies.
Certain fish had powerful fins with
arm bones like our arm bones,
and some could also breathe air.
Fish-like creatures developed fins with
many fingers and toes.
The first four-legged animals evolved.
Like frogs and newts, they were amphibians.

It was a great step in Earth's history
when our four-legged ancestors appeared.

▲ The fin of *Sauripterus*, a lobe-finned fish which lived in North America about
360 million years ago. This fin shows the origin of a feature that would prevail in all
land animals: three bones – the humerus, ulna and radius – in the arm.

▶ The skull of the placoderm fish *Gogonasus*, from Gogo in Western Australia, shows that some fish had only one pair of nostrils, like modern land animals. Such fish could probably breathe air.

▲ An evolution revolution takes place in a Greenland swamp, 370 million years ago. *Acanthostega*, seen here perched on a submerged log, has developed legs that it uses to crawl amongst the waterweeds. It retains the gills and tail fin of its fish ancestors and isn't yet capable of living on land. A school of young placoderms called *Remigolepis* swims past the *Acanthostega*'s tail while a predatory lobe-finned fish *Holoptychius* lurks in the background. On the distant shore we see the first forests, mainly composed of lycopods and ferns.

▼ Amphibians were the first group of four-legged animals to invade the land, after first evolving as water-dwelling creatures.

▼ The skull of *Ichthyostega*, an early amphibian from East Greenland that lived 365 million years ago.

◀ Ferns like this were among the first plants to colonise land, after mosses and worts. At this time, they were the most diverse of all land plants.

TODAY

1 000 000 000
years ago

2 000 000 000
years ago

3 000 000 000
years ago

4 000 000 000
years ago

5 000 000 000
years ago

6 000 000 000
years ago

7 000 000 000
years ago

8 000 000 000
years ago

9 000 000 000
years ago

10 000 000 000
years ago

11 000 000 000
years ago

12 000 000 000
years ago

330,000,000 years ago

Three hundred and thirty million years ago ...

Giant amphibians of many kinds
hunted in peaty lakes and marshes
where they laid their eggs to hatch as tadpoles.
The first reptiles laid hard-shelled eggs on land,
away from the jaws of hungry amphibians.
They hunted insects far away from the water's edge.
Giant millipedes sifted through leaf litter,
avoiding the poisonous tails of huge scorpions.

It was a great step in Earth's history
when reptiles first explored the land.

Large crocodile-like amphibians similar to the one whose skull is shown here dominated life on land 330 million years ago. This skull belonged to *Thoosuchus*, which lived in Russia about 100 million years later.

▲ On a forest floor of what will become Nova Scotia, Canada, the early reptile *Hylonomus* is chased up a lycopod tree by the large amphibian *Dendrerpeton*. *Asaphestera*, a smaller amphibian, scuttles into the undergrowth. Behind this drama, the huge millipede-like *Arthropleura* forages peaceably while one of the earliest flying insects buzzes overhead.

▲ The first land-living reptiles would have looked a lot like small lizards, such as this Thorny Devil from Australia.

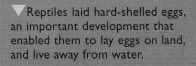

▼ Reptiles laid hard-shelled eggs, an important development that enabled them to lay eggs on land, and live away from water.

▲ The skull of an early amphibian, *Eucritta*, which walked on land about 330 million years ago in what is now Scotland.

▲ Euramerica is now a northern supercontinent.

1 000 000 000
years ago

2 000 000 000
years ago

3 000 000 000
years ago

4 000 000 000
years ago

5 000 000 000
years ago

6 000 000 000
years ago

7 000 000 000
years ago

8 000 000 000
years ago

9 000 000 000
years ago

10 000 000 000
years ago

11 000 000 000
years ago

12 000 000 000
years ago

260,000,000 years ago

Two hundred and sixty million years ago ...

Earth was cold.
Polar ice-caps covered the continents.
Reptiles, all sorts, lived on land,
and ate many kinds of food.
Some were warm-blooded
and grew tufts of hair that kept out the cold.

It was a great step in Earth's history
when animals could keep themselves warm.

▶ The skeleton of *Mesosaurus*, a small marine reptile that swam in the shallow seas of South America, China and South Africa.

▲ At the edge of a Russian lycopod swamp, a giant predatory *Eotitanosuchus* threatens a pair of bulky plant-eating *Estemmenosuchus*. A smaller predator, *Biarmosuchus*, watches from a rock outcrop.

▲ The skull of *Estemmenosuchus*, a strange-looking mammal-like reptile from Russia.

▲ The tooth whorl of a giant shark, *Helicoprion*, from East Greenland.

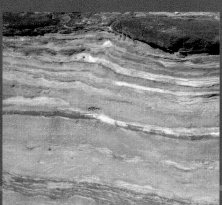

▲ Layers of 260-million-year-old sediment in Western Australia. The dark layers are rich in plant material that under pressure may form into thin seams of coal.

▲ Sea lilies or crinoids from the Gascoyne region of Western Australia. Huge colonies of sea lilies lived at this time in shallow seas around the world.

▲ The world as it looked 260 million years ago. There was now one giant landmass called Pangaea.

1 000 000 000
years ago

2 000 000 000
years ago

3 000 000 000
years ago

4 000 000 000
years ago

5 000 000 000
years ago

6 000 000 000
years ago

7 000 000 000
years ago

8 000 000 000
years ago

9 000 000 000
years ago

10 000 000 000
years ago

11 000 000 000
years ago

12 000 000 000
years ago

220,000,000 years ago

Two hundred and twenty million years ago ...

The Earth had one giant land called Pangaea.
Some reptiles walked upright on two legs:
they were the first dinosaurs.
Some reptiles had long fingers and leathery wings:
these were the first pterosaurs.
Some reptiles developed fish like-bodies
and lived underwater:
these were the first ichthyosaurs.
Some developed fur, special jaws, teeth, and they
became the first of our kind: the earliest mammals.

It was a great step in Earth's history
when dinosaurs and mammals first appeared.

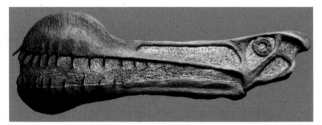

The skull of a pterosaur, *Tropeognathus*, from South America. Pterosaurs were the first backboned animals to take to the air.

The skull of one of the first known dinosaurs, *Herrasaurus*, from South America. *Herrasaurus* was an upright, walking predator about 4 metres long.

▶ *Kweichosaurus*, a small marine reptile from China.

◀ *Thrinaxodon*, from South Africa, one of the most advanced mammal-like reptiles. Such animals may have had hair and looked very much like a small dog.

▲ In an ancient forest in Argentina, pterosaurs dart overhead while the metre-long dinosaur *Eoraptor* (right) confronts *Exaraetodon* (left), a mammal-like reptile. Browsing behind them is a larger mammal-like reptile, *Ischigualestia*. Later, dinosaurs will dominate Earth and mammal-like reptiles will be rare – but they will also give rise to mammals.

▶ Fossil frog from Liaoning, China. Frogs first evolved 220 million years ago.

▲ Pangaea is the world's single supercontinent.

31

1 000 000 000
years ago

2 000 000 000
years ago

3 000 000 000
years ago

4 000 000 000
years ago

5 000 000 000
years ago

6 000 000 000
years ago

7 000 000 000
years ago

8 000 000 000
years ago

9 000 000 000
years ago

10 000 000 000
years ago

11 000 000 000
years ago

12 000 000 000
years ago

150,000,000 years ago

One hundred and fifty million years ago ...

In the seas huge reptiles called plesiosaurs ate fish.
Squid-like ammonites in magnificent coiled shells
swam next to 16-metre fish, feeding on tiny plankton.
Pine trees and ferns covered the land.
Long-necked dinosaurs like *Brachiosaurus*
grew to a monstrous 80 tonnes,
stegosaurs with armoured spikes quietly ate ferns,
and meat-eating dinosaurs chased and
slaughtered their prey.
Some dinosaurs grew long arms and fingers,
and sprouted feathers from each arm.
They climbed trees and flew bravely into the air.
They were the first birds.

It was a great step in Earth's history
when giants shook the ground and birds took flight!

Archaeopteryx, one of the first
birds, from Solnhofen, Germany.
Archaeopteryx has a skeleton
identical to that of other small
predatory dinosaurs, but has
enlarged arms with feathers that
were used as wings.

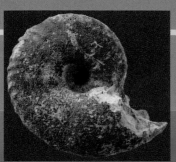

▶ An ammonite shell from Western Australia. Ammonites were squid-like animals that swam in buoyant shells.

▲ Portugal at this time was a land of giants. The stegosaur *Dacentrurus* takes a drink after filling its belly with plants. Predatory *Lourinhanosaurus* gives the spiny herbivore a wide berth while giant long-necked *Lusotitan* move gracefully in the background. In the air are two pterosaurs and *Archaeopteryx* (foreground), the earliest known bird.

▲ The saltwater crocodile can grow 7 metres long and is the largest reptilian predator alive today. Crocodiles first appeared 150 million years ago.

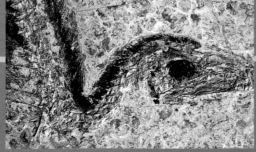

▶ The head of *Sinosauropteryx*, a small predatory dinosaur from China. Note the fine covering (in black) of simple hair-like feathers, demonstrating the close link between dinosaurs and the first birds.

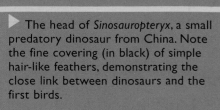

▲ Pangaea is breaking up into separate landmasses.

1 000 000 000
years ago

2 000 000 000
years ago

3 000 000 000
years ago

4 000 000 000
years ago

5 000 000 000
years ago

6 000 000 000
years ago

7 000 000 000
years ago

8 000 000 000
years ago

9 000 000 000
years ago

10 000 000 000
years ago

11 000 000 000
years ago

12 000 000 000
years ago

65,000,000 years ago

Sixty-five million years ago ...

Australia had begun to break away from Antarctica.
In the northern continent, herds of *Triceratops* grazed,
wary of the approach of a *Tyrannosaurus*.
Giant oviraptorosaurs watched butterflies suck nectar
from colourful flowers.
The first primate mammal played on a dinosaur skull.
Quetzalcoatlus, the largest flying animal ever,
flew across vast oceans in search of fish.

Then WHAM!
A huge meteor struck Earth,
causing floods, acid rain, and skies full of dust
that blocked the sun.
Some creatures died out altogether,
but birds, mammals, and other smaller creatures
survived.

It was a devastating time in Earth's history.

Triceratops, from North America, was one of the most abundant of the big plant-eating horned dinosaurs that lived right to the very end of the dinosaurs' reign. This skeleton is 8 metres long.

▶ The 1.4-metre-long skull of the dinosaur *Tyrannosaurus rex*, the largest predator on Earth at this time.

▶ Flowering plants, called angiosperms, had appeared and were flourishing by 65 million years ago.

▲ A snapshot of life in North America moments before the world was devastated by a massive meteor impact 65 million years ago. A tiny mammal scurries over the skull of a dead dinosaur, as an oviraptosaur approaches. *Triceratops* march in the background as the giant pterosaur *Quetzalcoatlus* takes to the air with its 12-metre wingspan.

▲ *Velociraptor* was a 1.5-metre-long, swift-running predator that lived in Asia and North America, and may have hunted in packs. It had large sickle-shaped claws on its hands and feet.

▲ How the world looked 65 million years ago. India is in the middle of the Indian Ocean, off Africa.

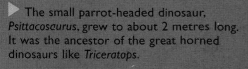

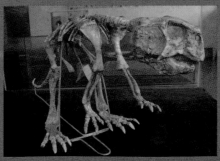

▶ The small parrot-headed dinosaur, *Psittacosaurus*, grew to about 2 metres long. It was the ancestor of the great horned dinosaurs like *Triceratops*.

1 000 000 000
years ago

2 000 000 000
years ago

3 000 000 000
years ago

4 000 000 000
years ago

5 000 000 000
years ago

6 000 000 000
years ago

7 000 000 000
years ago

8 000 000 000
years ago

9 000 000 000
years ago

10 000 000 000
years ago

11 000 000 000
years ago

12 000 000 000
years ago

40,000,000 years ago

Forty million years ago ...

The Earth was enjoying a warm climate.
Grasses and many kinds of trees appeared.
Mammals abounded: pouched marsupials,
egg-laying platypus, and many placentals,
which gave birth to live young
and nurtured them.
Some mammals gradually took to the sea.
These later became the dolphins and great whales.
Many kinds of birds flew in the air,
while giant flightless birds like *Diatryma*
hunted prey on land.
Huge penguins swam in southern seas.

It was a grand, green time in Earth's history
when the first grasses appeared.

A fossil *Grevillea*
leaf from Australia.
By this time, many
of the modern
plant families had
appeared.

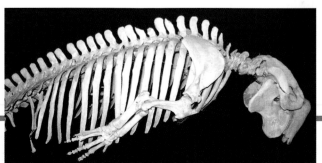

The skeleton of a
modern dugong. Mammals
took to the seas 40 million
years ago, and eventually
evolved into many kinds of
water-dwelling animals.

▶ The tooth of the largest killer shark that ever lived, *Carcharocles megalodon*, which grew to 15 metres long. The tooth is 16 centimetres.

▶ At this time, giant flightless hunting birds dominated the land. This is the skull of *Phorusrhacos*, which grew to about 2 metres high.

▲ In warm Antarctic seas, a mother whale, *Zygorhiza*, desperately tries to shield her baby from the monstrous 10-metre-long shark *Carcharocles auriculatus*. A pair of man-sized penguins called *Anthropornis* try to keep out of the way. Unlike their modern cousins, whales of this time still have small back legs.

▼ Some 40 million years ago, Australia was about to make its final break from Antarctica, ending the long reign of Gondwana as the dominant continent. All landmasses were shaped as they are today.

▲ The skull of a Tasmanian Tiger, a modern marsupial. Marsupials give birth to a tiny foetus which is raised in the mother's pouch.

▲ The rhinoceros is one of the largest land mammals alive today, next to the elephants. These are placental mammals which, like humans, give birth to well-developed live young.

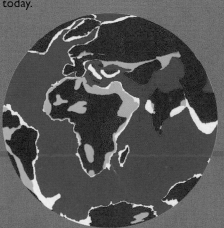

1 000 000 000
years ago

2 000 000 000
years ago

3 000 000 000
years ago

4 000 000 000
years ago

5 000 000 000
years ago

6 000 000 000
years ago

7 000 000 000
years ago

8 000 000 000
years ago

9 000 000 000
years ago

10 000 000 000
years ago

11 000 000 000
years ago

12 000 000 000
years ago

4,000,000 years ago

Four million years ago ...

Apes living in Africa came down from the trees
and walked upright on two legs.
We call them *Australopithecus*.
Their faces were flatter than other apes' faces,
their brains bigger.
They made excellent tools out of stone.
They were our ancestors.

It was a great step in the history of humankind
when apes left the trees to walk upright.

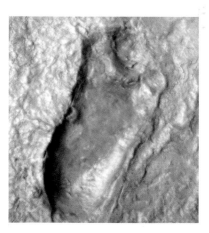

This footprint of an early upright walking
hominid from Laetoli, Africa, is about 3.5 million
years old. It was preserved in volcanic ash which
rapidly hardened.

About 3.5 million years ago, a land
bridge formed between North and South
America, allowing different animals to
cross between the two. Armadillos
originally evolved in the southern
continent, but today can also be found in
warmer parts of North America.

The skull of a 3-million-year-old ancestor of humans, *Australopithecus africanus*, from South Africa.

The skull of a gorilla, the largest living ape, differs mostly from us in its smaller brain size, thicker eyebrow ridges and larger teeth.

The skull, face on, of a baboon. Monkeys like the baboon appeared long before the great apes and have a more primitive-looking skull, yet we can still see a basic similarity to our own skull shape.

In Kenya, a group of apes called *Australopithecus anamensis* laze about in the afternoon. Unlike other apes, the australopithecines lack pointed canine teeth and walk upright, traits that will be kept in their human descendants, 4 million years later. Behind the apes is a herd of ancient antelope and what looks like a giant moose but is in fact the short-necked giraffe, *Sivatherium*.

An orang-utan, one of the living great apes. The chimpanzees, our closest living relative, diverged from the line leading to humans 7 or 8 million years ago.

A stone tool from Africa, 2–3 million years old. Our earliest ancestors had one great ability that no other animals possessed, to be creative and make things.

1 000 000 000
years ago

2 000 000 000
years ago

3 000 000 000
years ago

4 000 000 000
years ago

5 000 000 000
years ago

6 000 000 000
years ago

7 000 000 000
years ago

8 000 000 000
years ago

9 000 000 000
years ago

10 000 000 000
years ago

11 000 000 000
years ago

12 000 000 000
years ago

One hundred and sixty thousand years ago ...

Earth looked much as it does today.
People like us, *Homo sapiens*, had appeared.
They left their homes in Africa, began walking.
Eventually they spread to Asia, Australia, America.
They painted and carved on cave walls,
and made many clever tools.
They dreamed and imagined.

It was a great step in our history
when humans explored and settled different lands.

Cave paintings are the earliest forms of human art that we know of. Many of them depicted animals, and the artists may have believed that the paintings would help in hunting.

Stone axes like this Acheulian hand axe were in common use hundreds of thousands of years ago.

One of the oldest of the modern humans, Cro Magnon man, lived in France about 120 000 years ago.

As mammoths graze in the distance, a human compares an ivory bird-figurine to the real thing. Only a human would have the imagination and skill to turn a piece of mammoth tusk into the image of a bird. Over 30 000 years later, in the early twenty-first century, another generation of humans will discover the figurine at Hohle Fels Cave in Germany and they will marvel at its beauty and sophistication.

The skull of an early human, *Homo erectus*, that lived from 1.8 million years ago to about 60 000 years ago. It has a smaller brain size and more prominent eye ridges than we do.

The skull of *Homo heidelbergensis*, which lived in Europe about 400 000 years ago. This species was almost a modern human but still lacked our larger brain capacity.

TODAY

1 000 000 000
years ago

2 000 000 000
years ago

3 000 000 000
years ago

4 000 000 000
years ago

5 000 000 000
years ago

6 000 000 000
years ago

7 000 000 000
years ago

8 000 000 000
years ago

9 000 000 000
years ago

10 000 000 000
years ago

11 000 000 000
years ago

12 000 000 000
years ago

Today...

The continents are still slowly moving.
Weather and sea levels are changing,
as they always have.
We humans live in all corners of the planet,
sometimes in peace, sometimes at war.
We have walked on the moon,
and made amazing machines that allow us
to see and learn about the Universe.
But many animals and plants are dying out fast
because we take up more space for ourselves.

It will be a truly wonderful day on Earth
when we can live in harmony and peace
with each other, and with all other species.

1 000 000 000
years ago

2 000 000 000
years ago

3 000 000 000
years ago

4 000 000 000
years ago

5 000 000 000
years ago

6 000 000 000
years ago

7 000 000 000
years ago

8 000 000 000
years ago

9 000 000 000
years ago

10 000 000 000
years ago

11 000 000 000
years ago

12 000 000 000
years ago

+ 50,000,000 years ahead

50 million years from now ...

Australia will join Asia, and there will be one
supercontinent, Amasia.
Weather and sea levels will be very different.
New mountains and volcanoes will have formed.
Many animals and plants we know today
will have died out,
because of natural changes, or changes made by us.
New species will have evolved to replace them.
By then we may have built cities on Mars,
or colonised other planets in distant galaxies.
We might even have found the answer to the mystery
of how the Universe was formed.

The story of the Universe, ever-changing,
will go on, and on.

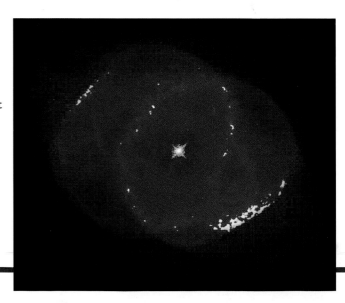

The 'Cat's Eye
Nebula' is a dying star,
or pair of stars, and
this picture is a visual
'fossil record' of what
it looked like 3000 light
years ago. In the
history of our
universe, 50 million
years is no more than
the blink of an eye.

▶ Erosion will continue to shape Earth's landscape, as it has done for millions of years.

▲ In the future, robots will probably be used for countless jobs that humans now do.

▶ Humans will continue to probe the far reaches of the Universe.

▲ On the surface of a strange world, great flying beasts battle in the skies while a great city glimmers in the distance. Could this be a world that humanity has yet to encounter? Or perhaps even our Earth in the unimaginably distant future?

Glossary

acanthodian (ack-anth-o-dee-an) • a kind of fish having spines in front of all its fins; now extinct

Acheulian • kind of hand tools made from stone being chipped away from a core, typical of sites between 1.5 million and 200 000 years old

Amasia (Amaze-ee-a) • a futuristic supercontinent that scientists predict will form in about 50 million years from now when Australia merges with Asia

amphibians • four-legged animals which breathe air as adults but have a larval stage, with the larvae breathing through gills in water. Amphibians include frogs, newts, salamanders and many extinct groups

arthropod • the group of animals with jointed legs that includes all insects, spiders, mites, crabs and other crustaceans, and many extinct groups like trilobites

asteroid • large rock in space, much larger than a meteoroid

Australopithecus (ost-ral-o-pith-ee-kuss) • Extinct genus of early hominid that lived in Africa 4-2 million years ago, directly ancestral to modern humans of the genus *Homo*

Big Bang theory • a theory that all matter came suddenly into existence through a huge explosion

coelenterate (sol-en-ter-rate) • simple animals with a radial symmetry like jellyfish, corals, sea anemones and sea pens

crinoid (cry-noyd) • a sea lily, a kind of starfish-like animal on a stalk

cyanobacteria • a kind of microscopic, plant-like cell which can bind grains of sand together to make stromatolites

dinosaur • one of a group of reptiles, often very large, that walked with their limbs upright (not with a sprawling gait like lizards or crocodiles); now extinct

Euramerica • a supercontinent that existed from around 550 to 250 million years ago

eurypterid (you-rip-ter-rid • a kind of sea scorpion, sometimes huge; now extinct

euthycarcinoid (you-thee-car-sin-oid) • a kind of segmented animal (arthropod) that had eleven pairs of legs; now extinct

Gondwana • An ancient southern supercontinent including Australia, South America, South Africa, India and at times other parts of Asia

Homo erectus, Homo heidelbergensis • species of extinct human which differ principally in their brain size

Homo sapiens • the modern species of human that we belong to

ichthyosaur (ick-thee-o-saw) • a kind of fish-like, swimming reptile with a long snout that lived in the seas at the time of the dinosaurs

lycopods (like-o-pods) • primitive plants with radiating rows of leaf-like structures; often called 'horsetails'

mammal • a type of warm-blooded animal with hair or fur that mostly gives birth to live young, except for primitive forms like the egg-laying monotremes (platypus and echidna)

mammal-like reptile • a group of reptiles that were similar to mammals in their jaw and teeth structure; now extinct

marsupial • a type of mammal that gives birth to young at a very undeveloped stage and nurtures the young inside its pouch (e.g. kangaroos, possums, koalas)

metazoan • any animal made up of many cells, not just one cell

meteor • streak of light seen in the sky when a meteoroid (a lump of space rock or metal) burns in the atmosphere; called a 'meteorite' once it has hit the ground

nebula • the remains of what was once a star after it has exploded

placental (pla-sent-al) • a type of mammal that keeps the young inside it until well-developed, then gives birth with the placenta attached (e.g. cows, whales, humans)

placoderm (plak-o-derm) • a kind of armoured fish with bony plates covering the head and body; now extinct

plesiosaur (please-ee-o-saw) • a kind of swimming reptile with long or short neck that lived in rivers and seas at the time of the dinosaurs

pterosaur (tear-o-saw) • flying reptile that lived at the time of the dinosaurs; now extinct

reptile • mostly cold-blooded, four-legged animals with scale-covered bodies – includes lizards, snakes, crocodiles, turtles and many extinct groups

Rodinia (Row-din-ee-a) • an ancient supercontinent that formed about 1 billion years ago and split up to form other landmasses, including Gondwana

sea pen • a feather-like structure built by a colony of coral-like animals (coelenterates)

stromatolite (strom-mat-o-lite) • layered sediment or rock structure made by cyanobacterial communities binding loose grains

supercontinent • ancient large landmasses that were made up of more than one of today's continental landmasses (e.g. Gondwana, Rodinia, Euramerica)

trilobite (try-low-bite) • a kind of sea-dwelling animal with jointed legs (an arthropod) and having the body divided into three parts; now extinct

Acknowledgements

The author would like to thank Dr Ken McNamara for checking the text, Brian Choo for his helpful advice, and Heather Robinson for help at every stage.

Brian Choo thanks Daniel Bensen, Stephanie Choo, Tracy Ford, Octavio Mateus, Andrew Williams and John Long for their valued assistance.

'There is in each of us...' on page 5 is an adaptation of words quoted by Professor Robert Hutchinson, formerly of the Natural History Museum, London.

Photography credits
pages 6–7 (all three photos) courtesy NASA – the Hubble Telescope
page 9 sun, bottom left, courtesy NASA – the Hubble Telescope
page 10 cyanobacteria, left, by Wim Van Egmond (www.micropolitan.org)
page 23 *Onychodus* skull, top, by Kristine Brimmell (WA Museum)
page 23 tiger shark, centre, by Clay Bryce (WA Museum)
page 27 dinosaur eggs, centre, by Glenn Martin
page 35 *Psittacosaurus* skeleton, bottom, by Glenn Martin
page 37 shark tooth, top left, by David Ward
page 38 armadillo from istock.com
page 40 cave painting from istock.com
page 42 astronaut, left, courtesy NASA, child painting, from istock.com
page 43 road, rice farmers, African, tiger and fern from istock.com; three children, right, by Tim Stitz
page 44 Cat's Eye Nebula courtesy NASA – the Hubble Telescope

All other photographs supplied by Dr John Long.

Index